A TREASURY OF AMERICAN BOOK ILLUSTRATION

A Treasury of

AMERICAN
BOOK ILLUSTRATION

by

Henry C. Pitz, 1895-

AMERICAN STUDIO BOOKS
AND WATSON-GUPTILL PUBLICATIONS, INC.
NEW YORK AND LONDON

TO MOTHER

ACKNOWLEDGMENTS

This book has been the result of many helping hands and minds. Many who never dreamed their ideas would appear in a book are here, like my friends, Edward Warwick, Leroy Wolfe and William Blood. Something is here from our many long conversations about illustration; something is also here from the shop talk of many of my fellow illustrators. It is the illustrators, of course, who have made the book. Many took great trouble to find and send me specific illustrations. Some, to whom I am particularly indebted, are Fritz Eichenberg, Constantin Alajálov, Warren Chappell, Robert Fawcett, Vera Bock, Roger Duvoisin, Clare Newberry, Frederick T. Chapman and Gluyas Williams.

The publishers have been almost uniformly kind in releasing work. Many editors have given largely of their time in making suggestions and hunting out original drawings or proofs. I owe a debt to Lillian Bragdon, Sabra P. Mallett, Rose Dobbs, Nancy Hunnekens, Sydney Jacobs and Arthur Rushmore for their great help. My thanks also go to George Macy for opening the riches of the Limited Editions and Heritage Clubs and to Morris Colman, Bertha Gunterman, Elizabeth Riley, Eunice Blake, Gertrude Blumenthal, Helen Frye, Barbara Chapin, S. Elizabeth De Voy, R. A. Freiman, A. P. Tedesco, Margaret Lesser, Ursula Nordstrom, Helen Ferris and May Massee.

A special acknowledgment is due Lucille Ogle for all the material she gathered and for her valuable assistance in preparing the offset color pages. Also for their help in the production of the book, acknowledgments are due to George W. Miller and Sam Faber.

Lastly, I must pay a tribute to my publisher, Bryan Holme. He has been enthusiastic and fertile in ideas and has taken on his shoulders the greater portion of the burden of all the many details that have gone into the making of the book.

THE AUTHOR

The spot drawing on this page is by FEODOR ROJANKOVSKY from "The Voyages of Jacques Cartier" by Esther Averill. (Domino Press).

Copyright 1947, Holme Press, Inc.

PRINTED IN THE UNITED STATES OF AMERICA BY PLANTIN PRESS AND WESTERN PRINTING AND LITHOGRAPHING COMPANY

★ THE ARTISTS INCLUDED IN THE BOOK ★

AMERICAN ILLUSTRATION

AMERICA is a land of prodigious appetites. It is young enough to want to taste everything and young enough to draw strength from even an injudicious diet. Its strong gastric juices triumph over the strangest brews and the most cloying mixtures.

It has a strong appetite for pictures, although this is yet to be discovered in certain quarters. For several generations that appetite has grown steadily, and just as steadily that demand has been satisfied, until today the average American lives surrounded with pictures. That does not mean, of course, that his home is filled with paintings, that he frequents the picture galleries and museums or that there is even a volume of the world's masterpieces on his living room table. But he consumes pictures as he makes his hasty strides through life. They often satisfy him for only a few moments and are then discarded. But he feels a great need for them. These pictures are his folk art, they are American illustration.

Illustrations flood the average American from all sides. There are the numerous magazines, large and small, designed to appeal to his dominant interests and more usual moods. These magazines pour from the presses each week, each month. There is the daily spate of newspapers, one in the morning and one in the evening. Mail brings him pictured circulars and catalogs and all kinds of cleverly designed advertising. As he travels he may scan with interest or resentment the billboards on his highways and the advertising cards in his trains, trolley cars or subways. There are pictures in his store windows and even the nightmarish neon lights sometimes take on pictorial form.

This may seem a strange way to satisfy pictorial hunger. But this is the twentieth century American's way, and if we hope to understand him, we must know something about the pictures that influence and delight him.

His insistent demand for a never ending stream of easily read pictures has brought into being a giant mechanism for their production and distribution. It is a mechanism of amazing size and power, built for speed and efficiency. The modern printing presses border on the miraculous. They run enormous editions of full color material at incredible speeds. The pressmen are intelligent, well trained and resourceful. The emphasis, however, is upon speed and size, not quality; consequently, the finest levels of printing and reproduction are seldom attained. Care, patience, and a high standard of craftsmanship do not, generally speaking, flourish in the American atmosphere. But if the highest levels are seldom reached, neither are the lowest.

The unique products of these presses are the large magazines—the great weeklies and monthlies of national circulation. They are without counterpart in the world of today. They are characteristically American. Their circulation, in the millions, blankets the country. They reach most of America's homes where they attempt to appeal to or instruct each member of the family, particularly the women.

The magazines carry a good deal of fiction. This fiction is rather on the bland side and is very much standardized. Only nice things are apt to happen in these stories and there is comparatively little danger of having one's heart wrung. Supporting this fictional window dressing is a large body of special articles and departmental material that attempts to cover the entire life of the American family. It offers guidance in health, dress, public affairs, the social amenities and community life. There are countless articles on the preparation of food, home planning and decoration, gardening, child behaviour and how to grow old gracefully. All this material is well-groomed and colorfully presented with a seemingly real sense of responsibility. Its influence is deep and important. The power of the great American magazines over American life and opinions should never be underestimated.

Today, almost all these messages first reach the American eye through a pictorial impact. The pictures that crowd the magazines are, among other things, bait to catch America's restless eyes. If those restless eyes can be halted for a moment by a splashing illustration, they may be lured into reading the text that surrounds it. So a great deal of American illustration is designed for momentary visual appeal. Too much of it goes no further.

The subject matter as well as the style of magazine illustration is usually as standardized as the magazines that carry it. It revolves about the two great characters of American fiction, the consistently glamorous American girl, who is often blonde, and the attractive well muscled American youth who stands at her side. He is often a little stupid, in a nice way, although sometimes he is very sharp and packed with magnetism because of an Irish grandmother. These two know how to dress. The illustrator is usually an expert at this sort of thing himself and the magazines have fashion consultants to help him. He is an expert, too, at surrounding his characters with a world of attractive tactile values.

It is easy to poke fun at run-of-the-mill magazine illustration, with its all too obvious weaknesses. It is less easy to see it in relation to the whole great world of American illustration, and to embrace that world in one clear glance, estimating both its power and its shallowness. It would be a mistake, too, to imply that there is only one kind of magazine illustration. There are brilliant exceptions among the illustrators and there are magazines that do not conform to the accepted pattern.

Observe the same type of slick picture making we have mentioned in advertising art. Here it finds an eager welcome for it exactly fits the needs of many advertisers. The field, however, is too large to be dominated by hundreds of smoothly brushed renderings of cuticle and dentine; this is only a part of a much greater thing.

The whole structure of advertising enterprise has expanded over the past twenty years with surprising rapidity. Its resources are dazzling, its funds appear limitless. It is alert to buy the best talent, the most talked of talent, the craziest talent. It supports an army of quick thinking young men who soon lose their capacity for taking a deep breath. It is the home of the human dynamo and the American live wire. It is both sophisticated and gullible. It is conscious of the molding influence it has on American life but is prone to worship its own statistics and surveys.

The simple act of selling something is the common denominator of all its motives, but it has thousands of ingenious ways of attaining that end. Make no mistake, it is crammed with intelligence, resourcefulness and invention. It has great stores of brilliance, and of hard common sense as well. It knows how quickly and effectively pictures can convey a message and it uses them in a big way.

JOHN JAMES AUDUBON from "Birds of America"—*Wild Turkey* (Above) and *Key West Dove* (Left). Published between 1827-1838.

"SMOKE GOT SOCIABLE WAYS, 'AIN'T IT?"

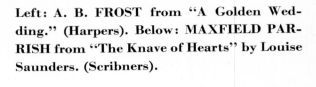

Left: A. B. FROST from "A Golden Wedding." (Harpers). Below: MAXFIELD PARRISH from "The Knave of Hearts" by Louise Saunders. (Scribners).

Left: E. A. ABBEY from "The Merry Wives of Windsor" by William Shakespeare. (Harpers).

The tens of thousands of pictures that advertisers buy each year represent almost every kind of picture making. Some are hack drawings, some are inspired; almost all are competent. Many of them are completely representational, others are more imaginative and sophisticated. Some advertising illustrators work with the finish of a Vermeer, others with the *joie de vivre* of Dufy. The newer movements in art have had their hearing too, for freshness and novelty also figure in the advertiser's scheme of things. Men are lured from the ranks of the painters and printmakers, artists are imported from abroad.

The result of all this is a rich mixture, greatly varied, highly spiced and stimulating. Its excitement communicates itself to the American public. By no means do they swallow it whole but they respond to it. They allow it to color their thinking and to influence their actions. It is a weapon of great potency.

All the branches of illustration have potency. The newspaper, which is so much a part of American life, is not renowned for its illustrations, but it has its political and sporting cartoons, which, no doubt, wield some influence. The Sunday issues carry a more elaborate pictorial display, but the magnet that draws the millions is the comic strip section. Weekdays in black and white, Sundays in the gaudy dress of Ben-Dayed color, it fastens its hold upon the *young* of all ages. The endless strips of inept pictures are often in the worst possible taste. Many readers shudder and throw them quickly aside. But something may be said for them. A few of the newer men have genuine gifts for picture narrative. The level is rising slightly. Even some of the more amateurish have a certain homely and gawky appeal. Perhaps they help to explain America. At any rate, only the most precious viewpoint would refuse to fit them into the huge frame of American illustration.

The last great category, and the one that concerns us here, is book illustration. It stands a little apart from the others. It wears a more permanent air and appeals to a quieter, more educated audience. Because of this, it is less standardized and offers greater freedom to its illustrators than do the other categories. Book illustration has become an art of rejuvenated energies during the past generation, for, during that time, America has become a book reading nation. It has also become what is popularly called "art conscious," and new groups of responsive artists, illustrators and designers have arisen to make American books attractive, often beautiful.

Not to be forgotten is the fact that illustration is also a teller of fairy tales for goggle-eyed children. Besides the old tales in period dress, a modern fairy princess may be a pretty stenographer who becomes a movie star overnight, and the prince a Western mining engineer. Even through such figures, the tradition of fairyland is preserved. People still believe in fairies, though sometimes the accessories must be brought up to date.

Although the separate categories of book, magazine, advertising and newspaper illustration exist, no one of them can be reviewed in complete isolation from the others, for the same types of pictures are found throughout. In fact, many illustrators work in two or three of these fields, sometimes in all of them. The categories interlock and together form a great popular art.

American book illustration is indeed a great art—abundant and fruitful—the sheer size of which the world has not seen before. Within its bulk are great complexities of method and interpretation. It has absorbed influences from all times and cultures and is still assimilating, still growing. Though it may spend much of its time in trivialities, it can say big things too. It has bounce and spring and great good health. It is glad to be alive.

THE ARTISTS WHO ILLUSTRATE AMERICA'S BOOKS

The artists who illustrate America's books come from the ends of the country or, in a larger sense, from the ends of the earth. The one thing they have in common is their talent—a talent not confined to any one soil or set of conditions. It comes from America, Europe, Asia; it comes from the farm and from the city; it may rise from a limited background or from one of ample opportunity.

America's illustrators spring from the numerous racial stocks that have settled in the land. Start calling the roll and you soon have a typical American list, comprising many racial backgrounds—Chappell, Lenski, Daugherty, Weisgard, Kent, Pène Du Bois, Wyeth, Gag, Stahlhut and Morgan. Then, besides the rich and varied backgrounds of our native born artists, are the even more diversified talents that have come to us more recently from almost every country in the world. Particularly during the years just preceding the war, scores of the finest talents of the globe were absorbed into American illustration. Even a short list of these names gives one a sense of the varied cultural impulses that are now uniting to form America's book illustration. From Russia, for instance, have come Boris Artzybasheff, Bobri, Feodor Rojankovsky, Constantin Alajálov, A. Alexeieff and Nicholas Mordvinoff; from Hungary, Willy Pogany, Marcel Vertès and Kate Seredy; from Sweden, Gustaf Tenggren; from Austria, Frank Dobias; from Germany, Fritz Eichenberg, Fritz Kredel and George Grosz; from Poland, Arthur Szyk and William Sharp; from France, Bernard Lamotte; from Mexico, Miguel Covarrubias and Carlos Merida; from England, Robert Fawcett and Clare Leighton; from Switzerland, Roger Duvoisin and Edgar D'Aulaire; and from Spain, Salvador Dali. These are only some of the artists from some of the countries, and American illustration has been enormously enriched by their work.

Most of the newcomers have found ample play for their talents. The machinery for book production here is considerably larger, and possibly more efficient, than elsewhere—and the book audience, of course, is the largest of any single country in the world. Nevertheless, our highest standard of printing craftsmanship usually still suffers by comparison with the best of many other countries; in fact, there is, if anything, a declining standard of artistry among our engravers and printers. Too often we think of engraving and printing only as industries, too seldom as arts or crafts. Consequently, our book illustrators cannot feel back of them the cohesive traditions that have bolstered the men of other countries.

Our picture making was still a young thing when the invention of photo engraving gave such sudden impetus to illustrated book publication, but in the period of little more than three generations a certain vaguely defined American style has begun to take form. Overnight, a company of very gifted men schooled themselves in the new art. Edwin Abbey, Howard Pyle, Walter Appleton Clark, Reginald Birch, Charles Dana Gibson, Frederic Remington, A. B. Frost and others helped to launch modern American illustration. Their influence is still felt. Of this group, Pyle, Gibson, Remington and Frost are unmistakably American. Their themes were mostly American and there is a certain homely quality to their work that reflected their country and their time. They were without benefit of foreign training and even the gloss of foreign influence is missing from their pictures. Their work, with the possible exception of that of Gibson, was solid and homespun rather than brilliant, but it reached intimately the audience of their time.

Howard Pyle's influence was the most important. Not only in his own work—those sincere and

HOWARD PYLE from "The Wonder Clock" with verses by Katherine Pyle. (Harpers).

convincing pictures of American history—but also in his teaching, where his solid but imaginative vision was reflected in the illustrations of many successors. For a generation after his death, his numerous students dominated the field. There was a large company of them. N. C. Wyeth, with his abundant pictorial health and love for the action and color of the world, was the natural successor to Pyle. He settled in the Brandywine country of Pyle and continued Pyle's celebration of America's past. His long series of colored illustrations of children's classics included a great variety of subject matter but it was into his American pictures that he poured his greatest love and understanding. The third generation of the Brandywine tradition is in the gifted hands of his son, Andrew.

The Howard Pyle students, Frank Schoonover, Stanley Arthurs, Jessie Wilcox Smith, George Harding, Edward A. Wilson, Harvey Dunn, Thornton Oakley, Elizabeth Shippen Green and others, were not only a company of prolific picture makers but also many of them taught illustration and tried to pass the Pyle tradition on to their students. They were probably successful in transmitting its essence, which was the important thing, although a superficial glance at present day book illustration actually reveals little trace of it. With few exceptions, in spite of the example of Pyle's own "King Arthur" and "Otto of the Silver Hand," they conceived illustrations that were to be tucked into books rather than to grow from the printed page. Only one of them, Edward A. Wilson, today creates important illustrations that are an integral part of the books they illustrate. But the Howard Pyle tradition is still alive, for the most part deep and underground and purged of some of its irrelevant trappings. The fact that it exists is chiefly important today because it represents the urge to tell the story of American things.

The young American illustrator can look back upon the brief background of his art and find much inspiration. The thoughtful ones are conscious of this background, but other hundreds are completely immersed in the popular picture making of the moment, thinking of illustration as the satisfying of transient fads and fancies. The book illustrator is usually largely exempt from these ephemeral pressures—the part he plays in illustration is of more lasting value. Because the material rewards of book illustration are, generally speaking, less than those of the magazine and advertising fields, he is not tempted to think of picture making only as a means of establishing the family fortune. He usually makes pictures primarily for the love of it and with the characteristic urge to contribute something new.

The basic training of the American illustrator has usually been acquired in one of the country's numerous art schools. Since the days of Howard Pyle's first classes at the Drexel Institute in Philadelphia, courses in illustration have multiplied rapidly. They vary from poor to excellent. Too many of them are vague in their planning and purpose, too many supplement the usual drill in drawing and painting from the model with a class in composition where only tentative attempts are made to focus attention upon current professional practice. Design is often neglected and reproduction presented inadequately or not at all. Insufficient attempt is made to bring the living world of illustration into the classroom. Illustration is not merely picture making, it is picture making with a sharp and definite purpose. On the other side of the balance sheet are excellent school courses handled by men experienced in the field and where professional practices are made as much a part of class routine as possible. However, nowhere in America is there, to my knowledge, a counterpart of the finest of the European schools, like the Academy for Graphic Arts in Leipzig. There the entire physical form of the book is studied. Type, paper, binding and printing are taken into proper consideration. A few of our native born artists like Lynd Ward and Warren Chappell have, however, had the benefit of that training and they, together with many of the artists arriving from Europe, have done much in raising the level of American book design. But most American artists in this field have learned book design the hard way, by trial and error. Their cumulative experience, nevertheless, is steadily piling up and making itself felt in all departments of book production.

It would be strange if book illustrators, like all other artists, were not devoted to their work. They love the printed word. They love the atmosphere of books, the feel of papers, the textures of bindings, even the smell of the printed page. In their struggle to produce fine work, they are often handicapped by budgets, poor paper and indifferent printing, but they are producing increasing numbers of exciting and beautiful books.

CHARLES DANA GIBSON

14

PICTURES FOR CHILDHOOD

Children's books present a land of opportunity and revelry for illustrators—the audience is eager and wonder-eyed and its editors alert and receptive. There is elbowroom for action, incentive for imagination and invention; there is more color to play with. The material dealt with is natural picture material. Sizes and shapes of books can often be unorthodox. No wonder the field attracts so many of the best illustrators. As a group, American children's books have flowered during the past quarter of a century into a brilliant renaissance. Their development parallels the development of all American book making, but to a considerable degree they have been leaders in that development.

Back at the beginning of the century, children's books were suffering from the same lack of functional design that affected the rest of the profession. But if the package left something to be desired, the contents were rich and substantial. Rudyard Kipling, Louisa May Alcott, Mark Twain, Joel Chandler Harris, Howard Pyle and Kate Douglas Wiggin, among others, were writing the stories. The same Howard Pyle, Reginald Birch, Peter Newell and others were making the pictures.

It seems inevitable, in reviewing the history of American illustration, to come back again to Howard Pyle. He was a giant to his contemporaries—a very much taller man then than he is now. The spectacle of him, pouring his best gifts into the writing and picturing of children's books, made all his followers view the field with the same high regard. His "Robin Hood" and "King Arthur" are milestones in children's book making. In their way they have never been surpassed.

Looking back, those earlier books had a completely Anglo-Saxon flavor. We were closer to English children's books then, closer to Alice, to Kate Greenaway, Beatrix Potter, Walter Crane and Kenneth Grahame. In the succeeding years came the infusion of many different foreign bloods that have brought about the cosmopolitan books of the present day. Place a Reginald Birch beside a Boris Artzybasheff or a Howard Pyle beside a Wanda Gag. The contrast tells much of the story. It is not that the Anglo-Saxon strain has dwindled. It still runs strong and deep, but it has been added to, blended and rejuvenated until the picture now is truly international. Sometimes the various cultural strains are clear and distinct, but more often they are merged and unrecognizable. This generation, like the last, is still one of assimilation. The digested result lies some time ahead.

The years that lead up to the brilliant present were filled with sincere and persistent work on the part of many persons and organizations. It was in 1893 that the first children's room was opened in a public library. A few years later, Anne Carroll Moore, as children's librarian at the Pratt Free Library in Brooklyn, began her important work for the development of young people's books. She edited the first children's book column and through her long life she has seen children's book rooms spring up all over the country and juvenile's book reviews multiply in the magazines and newspapers. For years now, there have been outstanding children's book columns in The New York Times and The New York Herald Tribune (for which Ellen Buell and May Lamberton Becker are now responsible), and the number grows steadily in the newspapers throughout the country.

For over twenty years, "The Horn Book," a magazine well edited by Bertha E. Mahony, has devoted itself exclusively to children's reading and pictures. "The Horn Book" was also responsible for an important "who's who" of children's illustrators entitled, "Contemporary Illustrators of

Children's Books," published in 1930. Now they have issued a much larger volume, "Illustrators of Children's Books." Another volume which contains many fine examples of children's book illustration is Howard Simon's "Five Hundred Years of Art and Illustration." The numerous children's magazines have also, of course, devoted space to books, beginning with the famous "St. Nicholas" and coming up through "The Youth's Companion" to the present day "Story Parade," "Boy's Life" and "Child Life."

Besides the growing literature on children's books, other activities have multiplied. Children's Book Week began in 1918 and has now become a period of important exhibitions and functions. It is an interval for appraising the year's output. There is a Newberry medal awarded each year for distinguished writing, and more important to the illustrator, the Caldecott medal for an outstanding picture book.

Another milestone was the formation of the Junior Literary Guild, in 1929, which still operates under the fine editorial leadership of Helen Ferris. By their monthly selections of outstanding books from all publishers (for different age groups), a tremendous impetus has been given to good children's books throughout the length and breadth of the land.

The worthiness of children's books lies largely in the hands of the children's editors. Almost all the important publishers have children's book departments and they are almost always presided over by women. They pick the manuscripts and choose the illustrators. They influence the design of their books. They are almost all able and gifted. It has been because of the wisdom and understanding of editors such as May Massee, Louise Seaman Bechtel, Lillian Bragdon, Ursula Nordstrom, Margaret Lesser, Lucille Ogle and others that children's books have reached such heights as they have at the present day.

Although the levels are high and the results stimulating, there is a danger signal. The making of children's books has become "big business." Many publishers no longer think of quality editions of five to ten thousand, they talk of a hundred thousand. Success brings its problems. Every inch of the earth's surface has been searched for material, so it would seem have the skies above and the waters beneath. Every *beastie* in the animal kingdom has been given his book. He has usually been given speech and thought, sometimes a sense of humor. Countless little native boys and girls from every country, province and tribal district have had their stories told. There is an endless stream of books telling how things are made, how things function and what makes things go. Every size, shape, format and binding possible for books has been tried. Books not only open, but they also fold, pop up, pull out, make noises, come apart and do other tricks. They have even come wrapped in such material as absorbent cotton and "bunnies" fur. This whole world of children's books is a very gay, bewildering and perhaps rather satiated world. It is difficult to say where new material and ideas can be found. Possibly a new and wise phase would be one of pruning and selection, of improvement of the old themes, of cultivating stories with more depth and of a generally higher level—while they yet remain light in essence and entertaining, giving the illustrator even more chances for the best expression of his talent.

The world of children's books is now a highly organized world. In it move battalions of progressive teachers, child psychologists and ardent librarians. They peer at the spectacle of a child reading a book with varying emotions—often with love and understanding, but sometimes with clinical eyes and therapeutic intent in their hearts. Sometimes they have no chastening humility before the wonder of childhood, and forget that reading and looking at pictures come under the heading of pleasure.

The illustrator has the better of it. Pseudo-psychology and pedagogy have laid light hands on him. He (or she) just makes pictures, but at the same time is usually very intelligent and genuinely interested in the texts of childhood. Unfortunately, many artists have enough conceit to think of the story merely as a vehicle for their pictures and when it comes to a pictorial test, a mediocre bit of writing may offer more picture opportunities than a gem of literature. Often, illustrators are secretly envious of writers. The thing appears to be so easy and the rewards so great. Among their own kind, they often say, "I'm going to try my hand at writing one of these days." And many of them do, frequently with splendid results. There are James Daugherty, Kate Seredy, Marguerite de Angeli, Wanda Gag, William Pène Du Bois, Nura, and Grace Paull for fine examples. It is, presumably, easier to collaborate with oneself than with another person, and the books these artists have written and illustrated are certainly important in the recent history of children's books. This is not to say that when the best writers, best illustrators and best printers do get together, the results are not the best because of course, more often than not, they are.

It is fair to say, however, that it has been the artists who have played the major role in making children's books the lively, beautiful and fascinating things they are now. There are some hundreds of them who have each played their large or small part in this development. Some, like Maud and Miska Petersham, James Daugherty, Kurt Wiese, Frederick T. Chapman, Diana Thorne, Dorothy Lathrop and Lois Lenski, have been active many years. Others are newcomers like Henry Stahlhut, Nicholas Mordvinoff, Clare Newberry, Henrietta Jones, William Pène Du Bois, Ilonka Karasz and Harold Price. To mention a few more, there are Vera Bock, Lynd Ward, Roger Duvoisin, Helen Sewell, Fritz Eichenberg, Lauren Ford, Gertrude Elliott, Allen Lewis, Ingri and Edgar Parin D'Aulaire, Manning Lee and Robert Lawson. The list could grow and grow. Each year fine new names could be added to it. One would have to be very presumptuous to pick any "fifty best" or "one hundred most distinguished."

When Boris Artzybasheff, over a decade ago, began his long series of decorated books, he brought a new and exciting element into book illustration. Artists and connoisseurs treasured little gems like his "Fairy Shoemaker" and 'Creatures." Most children could not accept them wholeheartedly, for the dazzling patterns bewildered them. But in "The Seven Simeons" (A Junior Literary Guild Selection), he achieved a book that captured all audiences. It is one of the most original and beautiful books of the last generation. Another milestone was Helen Sewell's "A First Bible."

More recently, Feodor Rojankovsky's "The Tall Book of Mother Goose," and "The Tall Book of Nursery Rhymes" and his pictures for "The Just-So Stories" of Kipling have reached a huge audience of children and grown-ups alike. These books were planned by The Artists and Writers Guild, an organization which has been responsible for a long list of outstanding books giving great circulation to the work of fine artists like Gustaf Tenggren, Cornelius De Witt, Rudolf Freund and Tibor Gergely. One of these groups, "The Golden Books" distributed by Simon and Schuster, is one of the most amazing book bargains of all time. Many of the fine ideas for content and format on these books were brought us from France by Georges Duplaix.

In a recent illustrator's competition held by one of the children's book publishers, hundreds of entries were received. A large proportion of these were of a remarkably high order of competence and originality, although many were the work of artists who had never illustrated a book. In spite of our present prodigal use of illustration, there is obviously a great pool of untapped talent in the country which indicates the enormous possibilities of future development.

THE GROWTH OF BOOK ILLUSTRATION

A generation or two ago, most book illustrations were just added to the books for which the publisher had ordered them. The originals were usually paintings or tonal drawings. They were reproduced by half-tone (like a photograph), printed on a coated (shiny) paper and tipped into the volume. A great many of these illustrations depicted the contents of the book with penetration and understanding but they had no physical affinity with the design or "make-up" of the book. They were as an afterthought and not part of the basic structure.

The conception of book making has changed a great deal since those days. We still have badly planned and poorly made books, and books in which the pictures bear no relation to the format or design of the pages. But they are no longer the accustomed thing. It is now safe to say that the majority of American books are well planned and a surprising number of them are fine examples of book design.

The designer and illustrator have shaken off the bewilderment brought about by the sudden invention of process engraving and the rapid development of modern printing processes. A surprising wealth of new effects was made possible in different printing mediums and it was natural that the illustrator should need time to study them and to experiment. At first, the new processes seemed to lead away from, rather than toward unified book making. In the twenties the tide began to turn noticeably. Good designers had always known that some of the very earliest illustrated books, like the Florentine chapbooks of the fifteenth century, were more beautiful examples of coherent design than most books produced with all the resources of the modern machine. They knew that type and illustration react upon each other and have to be organized by careful planning, that paper, binding, margin and spacing were parts of an allover pattern—each to be chosen or established with regard to the others. These things were not secrets. They had always been known, but their practice had been forgotten.

A few designers had this knowledge, like Bruce Rogers, Frederick Goudy and others, but at first they were lone voices. By the nineteen twenties, however, the forces that favored good design began to coalesce and a strengthened current of book production began to stream from the presses of America.

It is impossible to point to any single dominating force that brought about the change. There were many men, many organizations and many influences that combined to accomplish the quiet revolution that has brought us better books. For instance, the young firm of Alfred A. Knopf not only assembled a company of fresh and vital authors, many of them foreign, but they issued their works in volumes of excellent design. With the help of Elmer Adler and Will Dwiggins, the Knopf books became noted for their fine typography, unusual binding and generally attractive appearance. The Knopf imprint began to stand for fine format. Other alert publishers followed. Viking Press, with Milton Glick in charge of its design, became another important force, then came Oxford University Press, Random House and others.

The foreign presses of England, Germany, France and other countries had their influence. Work from such outstanding houses as the English Nonesuch Press and Golden Cockerel Press began to circulate in America and encourage our designers. Foreign designers like George Salter settled here and began to design books for American publishers.

In 1923, the American Institute of Graphic Arts assembled its first exhibition of "The Fifty Books of the Year." That first exhibition was a milestone. It gave American publishers a taste of what fine book making could be and opened the eyes of many to the considerable number of well designed books that were, in fact, already being produced. Represented in that first exhibition were many of the men who had pioneered in the cause of better books—Bruce Rogers, D. B. Updike, Walter Dorwin Teague, William Edwin Rudge, Edwin and Robert Grabhorn, Frederick Goudy, William Kittredge, Douglas C. McMurtrie, Norman Munder, Will Ransom, T. M. Cleland and Carl P. Rollins. "The Fifty Books of the Year" exhibition is now an annual event of great importance in the book world and a great spur to all intelligent bookmakers.

Through the twenties, certain printing houses, like the press of William Edwin Rudge, the Grabhorn Press and the Pynson Printers, began to be noted for high quality work. The university presses that now rapidly began to increase in number and importance, were invariably on the side of good printing. Also, the small private presses, like the Press of the Woolly Whale, of Melbert B. Carey, and Arthur Rushmore's Golden Hind Press, printing for the love of fine printing alone, were able to produce fresh and unusual things that were beyond the experience of most commercial publishers. All these things were adding to the rising tide of good book production. As the twenties passed into the thirties, beautiful books were no longer scattered exceptions.

All through the last two generations, the literature about book making has been steadily increasing. There is now available shelf upon shelf of excellent treatises on every phase of the book— the design and use of type, lettering and layout, illustration and the men who make it, printing and engraving processes, paper, binding, not to mention editing and estimating. For some years we had that fine journal of the book, "The Colophon," of Elmer Adler, and later "The Dolphin." Now the quarterly, *Print*, has been revived under the editorship of young William Edwin Rudge. "The American Artist," edited by Ernest Watson and Arthur Guptill, devotes considerable space to illustration, including a fine series on book illustrators by Norman Kent. Other periodicals are devoting increased space to book design and illustration while libraries and schools throughout the country constantly plan special exhibits of the printed page. The increasing quantity of literature and the number of public exhibitions are signs that interest in books and book illustration not only has become deep-rooted but is also growing.

It is easy to pile up the evidence. One of the most important clues is the amazing growth of the Limited Editions Club. Founded by George Macy in the midst of unpromising economic conditions, it has expanded to a startling degree. There is now a long and impressive list of books issued by the club and its associates, The Heritage Club and Junior Heritage Club. They are of varying degrees of excellence but the average is very high. A wide range of design and illustration has been used. Many foreign artists, like Hugo Steiner-Prag, Eric Gill, Robert Gibbings and Mariette Lydis have been introduced to the American audience. Native painters like Grant Wood, Fletcher Martin and Henry Varnum Poor have been given opportunities to make pictures for books. All these books have found a ready audience—that audience now seems to be a permanent thing.

A fine series of illustrated books is the more recent Limited Editions of Doubleday and Company, under the direction of Sabra P. Mallett. On its list of artists are Dali, Roberto Romano and Jon Corbino. Another series of great importance, not only because of the high standard of its design and illustration but also because this has been achieved at a remarkably modest price, is the Illustrated Modern Library. There are excellent volumes in this series illustrated by Allen Lewis, Boardman Robinson, William Sharp, Edward Wilson and Fritz Eichenberg. Another important venture is the Peter Pauper Press of Peter and Edna Beilenson. It has produced a long list of beautifully designed books—slender in bulk but spacious in treatment and moderate in price. Always enterprising in searching out new talent—this publisher had the first books of Aldren Watson, Sonis Roetter, Erica Gurecka-Egan, and Richard Lindner on their list.

The Rivers of America series, published by Rinehart and Company, is also illustrated with extreme versatility. Pictures for these books have also been made by a long list of distinguished artists including Stow Wengenroth, Frederic Taubes, Andrew Wyeth and Aaron Bohrod. Several new limited editions ventures are appearing, one of which is the revived Folio Club in Philadelphia. Pantheon Books, also comparatively new in the ranks of American publishing, have done a wonderful job in producing beautifully illustrated and designed books at a popular price.

These have been some of the good agents behind the book illustrator—and there have, of course, been others. They have provided him with opportunities which, naturally, he has seized with both hands, and with the result that he is now securer in the feeling that a truly receptive audience lies behind him. The field is, of course, crowded with hundreds of fellow artists, but the spirit of competition spurs him on to his best efforts. The presence in the American ranks of a growing number of artists from abroad gives him the chance to study at first hand the varied techniques and viewpoints of the entire world. All these things tend to make him alert, accomplished and versatile.

WINSLOW HOMER from "The Courtin'" by James Russell Lowell. (Osgood Co.)

THE BOOK PROPER

Book jackets are intended to take the soil and friction of early handling and sooner or later they show the marks of those encounters and are discarded. They are only an adjunct anyway, and the book proper is left. For those who have bought this book to enjoy the illustrations and wish to keep it as a treasury of some of the best work of the past many years, this section of the text may be of little or no interest. Nevertheless, in discussing book illustrations, something of the physical make-up and manufacture of the book should be discussed, as it is obviously so closely connected with the task that confronts the illustrator.

First come the covers within which the book is bound. Most American books are *case bound*— the *case* usually being two sheets of binder's board glued and united by some suitable binding material. The most common binding material is a cotton cloth, woven in varying textures and dyed in a large assortment of colors. It is most often covered with a starch filler or coated with pyroxylin. There are a great variety of other materials used less frequently—paper, of course, and silk, linen, brocades and other fabrics. There are a whole series of synthetic fabrics, some simulating leather and, finally, real leather itself.

What materials, what textures and what colors are to be used has to be decided between the publisher and binder and in the case of well designed books it is a matter of careful consideration and planning. Similarly, what design or type is to appear upon the binding must also come into this planning. Sometimes, nothing will appear upon front or back covers; frequently, a decorative spot of some kind; occasionally a large, full cover decoration or an allover pattern. But the *backbone* always calls for the title of the book, the author's name and publisher's imprint. This backbone is the narrow panel of binding we see when books are placed in their usual position upon a shelf and some element of identification is needed. Lettering and design is usually printed in gold or silver, or else in colored ink. Many designers consider the binding of much greater importance than the jacket, for it is a permanent thing, while the jacket is usually an ephemeral pictorial advertisement.

When we bend back the cover and open the book, we encounter a sheet of paper, half of which is glued to the back of the cover and the other half joined to the book proper along the binding edge. This sheet is the *endpaper*. It is structurally important because it furnishes the union between cover and book. In spite of the fact that it is frequently blank, it is often considered of aesthetic importance, too. Many designers seize the opportunity to say *welcome* to the reader by decorating the end papers. We have now opened the door of the book and we should be greeted by a feeling of invitation to go on further. After the assertiveness of the jacket, the endpapers can afford to be reticent and quietly persuasive. They are seldom treated as illustrations in the ordinary sense of the word, they are more likely to be stylized or decorative patterns. Often they are conceived in line and printed in a pleasantly toned ink on a tinted paper stock. They try to convey a hint, or perhaps more than that, of the atmosphere of the book itself.

The endpapers act as a bridge between the cover and the book proper. The pages which immediately follow, the so-called *front matter*, perform a variety of functions. They may contain a half title page (with the name of the book in small type), a frontispiece, title page, dedication and copyright notice page, acknowledgments page, contents page, list of illustrations, index, preface or introduction. These pages vary, of course, according to the requirements of the book and it is here that the designer may squeeze or expand a little, in order to bring the total page count of the book to a multiple of four for convenience in printing.* And to what extent they are decorated depends upon the designer. He may wish to be lavish or sparing.

The title page and the frontispiece (which faces it) are the most important "designed" pages in the average book. There was a time, not so many years ago, when a book seemed incomplete without a pictorial frontispiece. The pendulum of taste has swung, and today many designers leave it blank. When it is illustrated, it is usually designed in conjunction with the title page, its natural companion. The two are considered as a single unit, and it is essential that harmony be established between them.

Title pages are seldom the perfunctory things they were some years ago. Even when they are entirely a matter of type arrangement, they are planned with care and taste. The modern book designer has a great variety of different types (type faces) available to him—so many, in fact, that only when he wishes an unusual effect need he resort to hand lettering. We now have such an accumulated precedent of good book design, that even the designer who is not greatly gifted can, by staying close to the evidence about him, produce type arrangements of taste and style. And, if he wants to be inventive and adventurous, he has the pick of the best of the old type faces and a wealth of new ones which are at his disposal.

The illustrator usually likes to put a touch of his own upon the title page. If he is one of the younger school, he is likely to be familiar with type and hand lettering which is useful. Though he may not be an expert, he must nevertheless be no stranger to the world of printing processes. If he works in a technique that is susceptible to line reproduction, there is no great difficulty in obtaining harmony between picture and type. If his work requires half-tone reproduction (as in a photograph), there can never be quite the same intimate relation between the two, at least in letter press printing which usually requires half-tones to be printed on shiny coated paper. Only certain types of brush drawings can be reproduced by letter press (with a Ben-Day half-tone) on text (*antique*) paper.

The offset processes, no matter how much they may be decried by the book purists, do permit a more unified feeling between tonal pictures and type, for all illustrations can be printed on antique paper like the text itself. This may be purchased at the cost of sharpness of impression, but the fine *screens* (dot formations on the printing plate) give an allover softness that helps to tie illustration and text together. At any rate, offset is a printing method that must be reckoned with by the illustrator and designer, for it has become a strong rival of letter press—with the finer gravure processes, which achieve better texture, much less frequently used on account of cost. It should be noted that offset reproduction is particularly suited to the reproduction of pencil drawings. The Golden Books, with a large proportion of pages in color, are conspicuous examples of a high printing standard at a phenomenally low price, made possible by offset printing.

Once past the title page, the illustrator must work out his scheme for the heart of the book. The usual illustration is a full page picture, conforming exactly or approximately, to the size of the type page. That means that most book illustrations are upright rectangles, a serious handicap to some illustrators and a restriction for all. There are some men who do not compose readily in an

---

* According to the page size of the book, the size of the printing press and the quality of work required, sixteen, thirty-two or sixty-four (sometimes even ninety-six) pages are printed in one "form" at a time. Eight or four pages are also frequently printed if the accommodation of the text requires this or a quality job, such as color half-tone, is to be done.

upright shape, and even those who do, find at times that the subject matter, or the sheer need for variety, dictate a horizontal area. This, of course, can be obtained on the single page by cutting down the scale of the picture. Most headbands and tailpieces are of this type. But if the illustrator wishes a large, expansive effect he must lap over both pages.

This also brings its problems. The center fold, where the two pages meet, is always an obstacle for it splits the picture, even when the illustration is designed to run down into the gutter of one page and up and across the other. The double page illustration can only be continuous when printed on the two center pages of any *signature* (the center pages of a folded eight or sixteen page form). In all other positions, the plate must be broken and only great care, practically impossible in mechanical binding, will bring the halves into perfect alignment in the finished book. Even then, of course, the fold of the page arrests the eye.

The continuous double page picture is only sometimes the solution. Mechanical and aesthetic reasons often persuade the artist to make a split in the two parts of his picture; in short, not to gloss over the junction of the pages. No matter what course he follows, he must solve the neat compositional problem of designing a unified picture without undue violence to the whole or to either part in the event it is cut in half by a fold.

The beginnings and ends of chapters are natural places for decoration, and many books are illustrated by this means alone. It is a traditional scheme of book decoration. Some illustrators, feeling that chapter heads and endings, even if only treated typographically, are natural breaks in the monotony of type pages, prefer to scatter their smaller illustrations through the body of each chapter. Other artists or designers prefer an informal scheme—small, spontaneous drawings, usually of the vignetted kind, spaced deftly throughout the book.

Distribution is always an important factor in any scheme of book illustration. The pictures should fall at fairly even intervals, not in clumps with long deserted stretches between. This principle can be a bother to the illustrator, for the points of pictorial interest in the text are seldom spaced evenly, and he is often forced to picture incidents which do not move him greatly. Of course, there is no unanimity among illustrators as to what constitutes pictorial interest. Literally, one man's meat is another man's poison. Each artist's particular limitations narrow his vision when surveying a new text. What one man fumbles, another turns into a pictorial triumph.

The whole problem of fitting stories to the proper illustrators is a fascinating, but at times, very difficult one. It is an ever present problem with the book editors—some solve it amazingly well, others perfunctorily. The story is settled upon first, then the illustrator must be fitted to it. The better illustrators, being in considerable demand, are not always available—besides the perfect illustrator does not really exist. Each one has his strength and his weakness. Even the best are less accomplished in certain directions. There are numerous men among the illustrators, for instance, who are unable to portray a woman with real conviction. There are numerous women illustrators whose male characters are clothes and sawdust. The men are usually inept at drawing very young children—the women usually excellent. There are some illustrators who do brilliant pen and ink, yet half their power evaporates in a tonal drawing. Some are natural black and white artists; others are natural colorists.

In short, few artists are armed at all points. But the average picture-loving public has not discovered that. They believe their favorite illustrators, whoever they may be, can do everything from elephants to shiny new automobiles, from lovely ladies to cuddly kittens. Their faith is wonderful, but at times embarrassing. Some editors share this faith and the illustrator is often regarded

23

as a jack-of-all-trades. Sometimes, of course, he is—or comes to believe that he is. In any event, book illustration breeds versatility and, on the whole, probably never before has there been such a large body of talent that could do so many things so exceedingly well.

The competitive side of illustration exacts a penalty too, for it tends to make opportunists of the less successful men. They become eager to take any kind of pictorial gamble in the hopes of turning up an adequate response. And the successful ones, pressed by publishers and their own ambitions, work rapidly and continuously. They seldom have time for meditation, appraisal and renewal. All creative natures need to lie fallow at intervals—the illustrator is continually scratching up his crops before they are half grown.

All this may sound like a dismal life for one to elect of his own free will but it is not—not to the illustrator. He may grumble and complain in his weaker moments, but he loves the stimulation of constant effort, the procession of new and unexpected problems, and even the midnight sessions over the drawing board. He always believes his next picture will be his best—the next book, the perfect one. He even loves deadlines and quarrels with the engraver. No doubt about it—the illustrator is a special breed of artist.

ROCKWELL KENT from his book "N by E." (Brewer and Warren).

24

BOOK JACKETS

Book jackets hardly come into a survey of book illustration because ordinarily they come under the heading of posters or package designs. Therefore, with the exception of a few incidental examples which represent borderline cases, they are not covered in the illustrated section of this book. A few brief notes about them, however, may be interesting to some readers.

Dust covers, or book jackets, are a necessary part of the modern American book. Once, they were merely sheets of paper wrapped around the covers to protect them from casual handling, now they are embellished beyond the dreams of their originators. They still perform their early function but since the publisher has discovered that they sell his books, time, money and ingenuity are now lavished upon them.

The American producer has found that attractively packaged goods sell better, and books are no exception. More people than one would believe come to the book counters with no definite purchase in mind. They are prepared to reach for whatever attracts their roving eyes. If a jacket can impel people to hestitate, look and examine, it has done all that most publishers ask of it. Most designers ask a little more. They would have it perform its commercial function while remaining a well conceived design, a thing of beauty. Often it satisfies both demands.

The designing of a book jacket poses no mean problem for the artist. It is a complex thing. It should beckon the possible purchaser from a reasonable distance with some of the carrying power of a poster. It should also appeal when held in the hand. By utilizing all the resources of design, the contents of the book should be summed up and its general flavor imparted to the beholder. The title and author's name should be incorporated into the design and the lettering should be both legible and attractive. Most of the problems that are likely to confront the illustrator are concentrated in the book jacket.

Yet, highly specialized as the book jacket is, there are few designers who devote a major portion of their time to it. For one thing, it is, by and large, a rather unremunerative field. Besides this, in the publisher's constant search for novelty and surprise, there is incessant reaching for new talent and for fresh effects.

This reaching for new talent opens the door to the young aspirant. No inconsiderable number of the year's jackets are designed by artists fresh from school or in the beginning years of their professional careers. These artists bring their youth and eagerness to the problem. They are usually given books, the profit making possibilities of which are dubious—books by new writers, or by experienced writers whose sales have been small. The publisher wishes to keep his costs to a minimum. He gives the artist a small fee and asks for a design that may be reproduced simply, perhaps in two or three flat colors. As a result, some of these jacket designs are mediocre and technically inept, but many are fresh and inventive. The continuous flow of young talent, however, keeps the field invigorated. An exhibition of an entire year's output of American book jackets would contain many banal and wrongly conceived designs but the general effect would be colorful, lively and exciting. A select show of the "fifty best" is held by The National Arts Club in New York each year and is judged by a jury of art critics, which shows the seriousness with which jacket design is now taken, artistically speaking.

The better types of books are likely to gravitate toward the more established artists. Their fees are larger, more is expected of them and most of the better designs come from their brushes. The jackets requiring a pictorial display go to the illustrators and those needing a typographical solution are done by skilled book designers. The jackets of illustrated books are, of course, almost invariably drawn by the illustrator himself.

With the emphasis laid upon novelty and the power of attraction, there is a natural temptation toward excess. Colors are often more positive and blatant than they need be, the designs more violent. In other words, shrieks are more common than whispers; too much is sacrificed to momentary effects. But amid so much action and assertiveness, a quiet demeanor stands out in contrast. Many publishers are alive to this and utilize an interesting change of pace in their jacket campaigns. Although it is a lively field, and most types of graphic presentation are to be found within its borders, it obeys certain laws and follows certain habits. The average person will unconsciously gauge the type of contents of a book by its jacket. That is the way most jackets are planned to operate. Take, for instance, standard mystery stories. The jackets brand them. The accessories of crime and detection are there—the darkly silhouetted figure, the menacing shadows, the smoking gun and the spreading red stain. A few years ago, these motifs were handled in a highly realistic way. Now the influence of modern art is felt—more here, for some reason, than in any other type of book. Most are stylized designs, often quite abstract in form. The little chill of terror that they are supposed to evoke comes more often from the cunning use of spaces, rhythms and dark colors than from the careful depiction of objects. But mysteries are a group that, with a few exceptions, are instantly identifiable by their jackets.

Another group is the light, summer type of novel which has a jacket as sentimental and conventional as its contents. It usually calls for a full color painting of the naturalistic school. At the other extreme is the smart, sophisticated or risqué tale. A jacket for this type will usually contain echoes of the French moderns or the "Vogue" or "The New Yorker" school of draughtsmanship.

That unique American product, the "Western," almost always has a pictorial jacket. The original is usually a full color painting laid in with fat brush strokes, sunny in color, and vigorous in action. The historical romance is also usually pictorial, but more finished, more inclined to be decorative and sometimes a little more original in layout. Other classes of fiction are more difficult to classify. Usually, the more literary a novel, the less likely is it that the jacket will receive pictorial treatment. Carefully planned typography and small, well considered decorative elements are a frequent solution. This same treatment is often applied to the historical or biographical book. The beauty of much of today's type design and hand lettering can be seen in these latter groups.

Children's book jackets, of course, give the maximum opportunity for color, gay effects and inventive design. Their varied shapes invite the designer and the picturesque material with which they usually deal delights his picture making soul. He can approach the problem with a light heart. As in every other group there are poor ones and excellent ones but, on the whole, they comprise the gayest and most exciting group of all.

A collection of contemporary book jackets serves as an interesting barometer of America's interests and taste. One can easily imagine a scholar of a hundred years hence, poring over them with fascination. They will carry the flavor of our age as effectively as the Victorian valentines or the early English chapbooks do theirs.

PAUL McPHARLIN from "The Rubaiyat of Omar Khayyam," Fitzgerald version. (Peter Pauper). Right: SARKIS KATCHADOURIAN from "The Rubaiyat of Omar Khayyam," Fitzgerald version. (Grosset and Dunlap). Below: Projected illustration by BOBRI for "The Rubaiyat of Omar Khayyam." Below right: HELEN SEWELL. Spot drawing from "Ten Saints" by Eleanor Farjeon. (Oxford University Press).

LYND WARD from "For Whom the Bell Tolls" by Ernest Hemingway. (Limited Editions). Left: JAMES DAUGHERTY from "King James' Bible," designed by Richard Ellis. (Didier). Below: JAMES DAUGHERTY from his book, "Abraham Lincoln." (Viking).

Circe's Palace

Projected illustrations by DANIEL RASMUSSEN for "Tanglewood Tales" by Nathaniel Hawthorne.

Pomegranate Seed

E. McKNIGHT KAUFFER from "Green Mansions" by W. H. Hudson. (Modern Library, Random House).

HANS JELINEK from "Rip Van Winkle's Dream" by Jeannette Michael Haien. (Doubleday). Below: PAUL LANDACRE from "Tales of Soldiers and Civilians" by Ambrose Beirce. (Limited Editions).

32

STEELE SAVAGE from "Mythology" by
Edith Hamilton. (Little, Brown).

MIGUEL COVARRUBIAS. Top, left and top of opposite page: from his book, "Mexico South." and (Below): from his "Island of Bali." (Knopf).

Huaves of
San Mateo del
Mar

Right: C. LEROY BALDRIDGE from "Hajji Baba" by Franz Werfel. (Random House). **Below: NICHOLAS MORDVINOFF** from "Pépé Was the Saddest Bird" by William Stone. (Knopf).

I T was late in November, 1456. The snow fell over Paris
with rigorous, relentless persistency; sometimes the wind
made a sally and scattered it in flying vortices; sometimes
there was a lull, and flake after flake descended out of the
black night air, silent, circuitous, interminable. To poor people,
looking up under moist eyebrows, it seemed a wonder where it all
came from. Master Francis Villon had propounded an alternative
that afternoon, at a tavern window: was it only Pagan Jupiter
plucking geese upon Olympus? or were the holy angels moulting?
He was only a poor Master of Arts, he went on; and as the question
somewhat touched upon divinity, he durst not venture to conclude.
A silly old priest from Montargis, who was among the company,
treated the young rascal to a bottle of wine in honor of the jest and
grimaces with which it was accompanied, and swore on his own
white beard that he had been just such another irreverent dog
when he was Villon's age.

The air was raw and pointed, but not far below freezing; and
the flakes were large, damp, and adhesive. The whole city was
sheeted up. An army might have marched from end to end and
not a footfall given the alarm. If there were any belated birds in

BARBARA CRAWFORD from "R. L. S." three famous stories by Robert Louis Stevenson. (Folio Club).
Below: MARYA WERTEN from "Marta the Doll" by Eloise Townsbury. (Longmans, Green).

1

2

DALE NICHOLS from his book, "A Philosophy of Aesthetics." (Black Cat). Above right: VERA BOCK. Spot drawing from "A Ring and a Riddle" by M. Ilin and E. Segal. (Lippincott). Below left: SUZANNE SUBA from "The Cat" by Colette. (Farrar and Rinehart). Below right: ROCKWELL KENT from "Leaves of Grass" by Walt Whitman. (Heritage).

Right: JOHN THOMASON from "Adventures of General Marbot," edited by John Thomason. (Scribners). Left: WILL JAMES from his book, "The American Cowboy." (Scribners). Bottom: PAUL BROWN from "Cavalry Mount" by Fairfax Downey. (Dodd, Mead).

Opposite Page, top: MARGUERITE DE ANGELI from her "Bright April." (Doubleday). Bottom: JULIEN BINFORD. Jacket design for "Romance for Rosa" by Rachel Varble. (Doubleday).

HAROLD PRICE from "Paji" by Esther Kiviat. (McGraw-Hill). Below left: JEAN CHARLOT from "The Book of Christopher Columbus" by Paul Claudel. (Yale University Press). Below right: GUSTAF TENGGREN from "Tenggren's Story Book." (Simon and Schuster). Opposite Page, top left: MARIE LAWSON from her book, "Dragon John." (Viking). Top right: CARLOS MERIDA from "The Hungry Moon" by Patricia Fent Ross. (Knopf). Bottom: FEODOR ROJANKOVSKY from "The Tall Book of Mother Goose" and "The Tall Book of Nursery Tales." (Harpers).

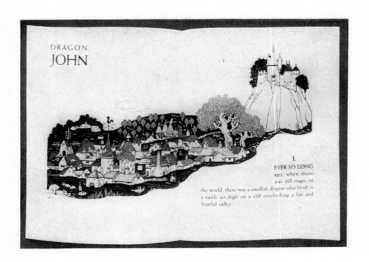

VALENTI ANGELO from "The Song of Roland," translated by Charles Scott Moncrieff. (Limited Editions). Center: ALLEN LEWIS. Frontispiece and title page from "Ivanhoe" by Sir Walter Scott. (Limited Editions). Bottom: MIGUEL COVARRUBIAS from "The Conquest of Mexico" by Captain Bernal Diaz del Castillo. (Limited Editions).

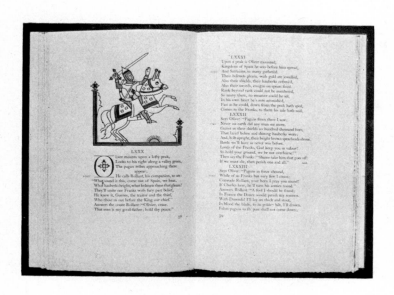

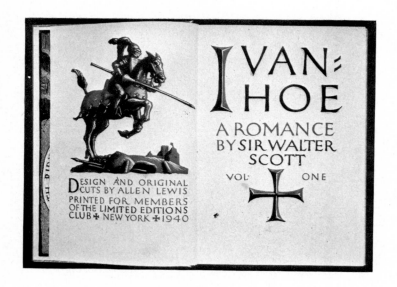

HELEN SEWELL from "A Book of Myths,"
selected from Bulfinch's "Age of Fable."
(Macmillan).

43

VERA BOCK. Spot drawing for "Love's Enchantment" by Helen Ferris. (Doubleday). Above right: EMLEN ETTING from "Amerika" by Franz Kafka. (New Directions). Below: ALDREN WATSON from "Honorable Goat" by Helen Cory Bliss. (Crowell).

44

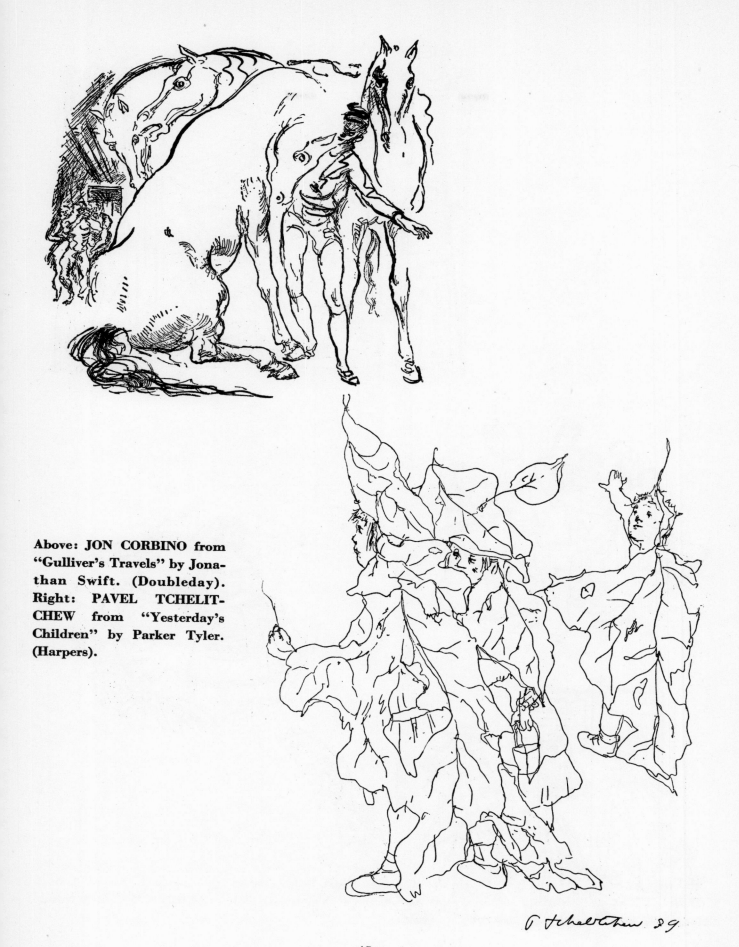

Above: JON CORBINO from "Gulliver's Travels" by Jonathan Swift. (Doubleday). Right: PAVEL TCHELITCHEW from "Yesterday's Children" by Parker Tyler. (Harpers).

46

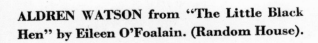

ALDREN WATSON from "The Little Black Hen" by Eileen O'Foalain. (Random House).

Opposite Page:

SHEILAH BECKETT from "The Gondoliers," Gilbert and Sullivan, adapted by Robert Lawrence. (Grosset and Dunlap).

47

JOSEF SCHARL

from "Grimm's Fairy Tales." (Pantheon).

Top left and bottom left: MARGERY
BIANCO from "Franzi and Gizi" by Gisella
Loeffler. (Messner). Above: ILSE BISCHOFF
from "In Calico and Crinoline" by Eleanor
Sickels. (Viking). Below: LOIS LENSKI from
"The Donkey Cart" by Clyde Robert Bulla.
(Crowell).

Above: GERTRUDE ELLIOTT from "The Golden Book of Poetry" selected by Jane Werner. (Simon and Schuster).

Right: LEONARD WEISGARD from "The Golden Egg Book" by Margaret Wise Brown. (Simon and Schuster).

HELEN SEWELL from "A First Bible," Edited by J. W. Maury. (Oxford University Press).

CONSTANTIN ALAJALOV from *"Cinderella"* by Alice Duer Miller. (Coward-McCann).

C. LEROY BALDRIDGE from "Translation from the Chinese" by Arthur Waley. (Knopf). Right: CARLOS MERIDA from "The Hungry Moon" by Patricia Fent Ross. (Knopf). Opposite Page: RUDOLF FREUND from "American Butterflies and Moths" by Cecile Matschat. (Random House).

55

A. ALEXEIEFF

from "Russian Fairy Tales," translated by
Norbert Guterman. (Pantheon).

ILONKA KARASZ from "The Heavenly Tenants" by William Maxwell. (Harpers).

Opposite Page:

WANDA GAG. Above: from "Three Gay Tales from Grimm." Left: from "Snow White and The Seven Dwarfs". Below: from her book, "Snippy and Snappy." (Coward-McCann).

Opposite Page, top left: HAROLD VON SCHMIDT from "December Night" by Willa Cather. (Knopf). Top right: FRITZ EICHENBERG from "Mistress Masham's Repose" by T. H. White. (Putnam). Below, left and right: STANISLAV BOBINSKY from his book, "In Voytus' Little House." (Roy). Above: FRITZ EICHENBERG from "Gulliver's Travels" by Jonathan Swift. (Heritage). Right: RENÉ D'HARNONCOURT from his book, "Mexicana." (Knopf).

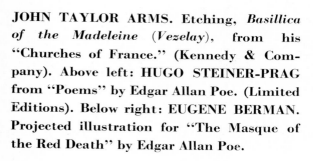

JOHN TAYLOR ARMS. Etching, *Basillica of the Madeleine (Vezelay)*, from his "Churches of France." (Kennedy & Company). Above left: HUGO STEINER-PRAG from "Poems" by Edgar Allan Poe. (Limited Editions). Below right: EUGENE BERMAN. Projected illustration for "The Masque of the Red Death" by Edgar Allan Poe.

Opposite Page:

ALLEN LEWIS from "Made in India" by Grace Yaukey. (Knopf). Below: FRITZ EICHENBERG from "Wuthering Heights" by Emily Brontë. (Random House).

Top left: SHEILAH BECKETT from "The Mikado," adapted by Robert Lawrence from Gilbert and Sullivan's opera. (Grosset and Dunlap). Above: LEONARD WEISGARD from "Louis of New Orleans" by Francis Cavanah. (McKay). Left: LUCILLE CORCOS from "A Treasury of Gilbert and Sullivan," edited by Deems Taylor. (Simon and Schuster).

LEONARD WEISGARD from "Under the Greenwood Tree" by William Shakespeare. (Oxford University Press). Right: HELEN SEWELL from "Ten Saints" by Eleanor Farjeon. (Oxford University Press). Below: NAOMI AVERILL from "The Story of the Middle Ages" by Donald Culross Peattie. (Grosset and Dunlap).

FRITZ KREDEL from "H.M.S. Pinafore," adapted from Gilbert and Sullivan by Opal Wheeler. (Dutton). Below: ERICA GURECKA-EGAN from "Turkish Fairy Tales" by Ignacz Kunos. (Peter Pauper).

ROGER DUVOISIN from his book, "The Three Sneezes." (Knopf).

PEGGY BACON from "Rootabaga Country" by Carl Sandburg. (Harcourt, Brace). Left: CHARLES B. WILSON from "The Champlain" by Louise Hall Tharp. (Little, Brown).

ASA CHEFFETZ from "Almanac for Moderns" by Donald Culross Peattie. (Limited Editions). Below: **JAMES DAUGHERTY** from "Courageous Companions" by Charles J. Finger. (Longmans, Green).

Edward Shenton

EDWARD SHENTON from "The Year-ling" by Marjorie Kinnan Rawlings. (Scribners). Left: FRED LUDEKENS from "Ghost Town" by G. Ezra Dane. (Knopf). Opposite: ROBERT FAWCETT from "Young Hickory" by Stanley Young. (Rinehart).

To Grahame Cage.   Alec Saurers

Top left: ALDREN WATSON from "Miss Pennyfeather and the Pooka" by Eileen O'Faolain. (Random House). Above: STEELE SAVAGE. Headpiece from "Mythology" by Edith Hamilton. (Little, Brown). Below: HANS ALEXANDER MUELLER from "A Tale of Two Cities" by Charles Dickens. (Folio Club).

LYND WARD from "Les Miserables" by Victor Hugo (Heritage) and (Bottom left) from his book "Vertigo," a novel in woodcuts. (Random House).

73

MARCEL VERTÈS from his book, "Art and Fashion" (American Studio Books) and (below) projected illustration for a dog story.

CORNELIUS DEWITT *from* "The Golden Encyclopedia" *by Dorothy A. Bennett. (Simon and Schuster).*

FEODOR ROJANKOVSKY from "The Ugly Duckling" by Hans Christian Andersen. (Grosset and Dunlap).

FEODOR ROJANKOVSKY from "The Ugly Duckling" by Hans Christian Andersen. (Grosset and Dunlap).

THE WALT DISNEY STUDIO from "Pinocchio," told by Dorothy Walter Baruch. (D. C. Heath).

MARY PETTY from "Good-bye, Mr. Chippendale" by T. H. Robsjohn-Gibbings. (Knopf).

FEODOR ROJANKOVSKY

from "The Voyages of Jacques Cartier," retold by Esther Averill. (Domino Press).

UMBERTO ROMANO from "The Divine
Comedy" by Dante Alighieri. (Doubleday).

VERA BOCK from "Love's Enchantment" by Helen Ferris. (Doubleday). Below: LAUREN FORD from her book, "Ageless Story." (Dodd, Mead).

Left: CLARE T. NEWBERRY from her book, "Babette." (Harpers). Below: MIGUEL COVARRUBIAS from his book, "Mexico South." (Knopf).

84

JOEP NICOLAS from "The Romance of Tristan and Iseult," retold by Joseph Bédier. (Pantheon).

ROCKWELL KENT

from "Moby Dick" by Herman Melville. (Doubleday).

CLARE LEIGHTON. Two illustrations from
"The Time of Man" by Elizabeth Madox
Roberts. (Viking).

Opposite Page: ROCKWELL KENT from
"The Complete Works of Shakespeare,"
edited by William Aldis Wright. (Doubleday).

WARREN CHAPPELL from "A Connecticut Yankee in King Arthur's Court" by Mark Twain. (Heritage). Left: LYLE JUSTIS. Projected illustration for a book on Napoleon.

GARTH WILLIAMS from "Stuart Little" by E. B. White. (Harpers). Below: DONALD McKAY from "Barchester Towers" by Anthony Trollope. (Doubleday).

BERNARD LAMOTTE from his book, "Oil Painting and Brush Drawing." (American Studio Books).

LUDWIG BEMELMANS from his books:
"The Blue Danube" (Above) and "Made-
line" (Right). (Viking).

CANDIDO PORTINARI from "Maria Rosa" by Vera Kelsey. (Doubleday). Below: N. C. WYETH from "Drums" by James Boyd. (Scribners).

Opposite Page:

WARREN CHAPPELL from "Don Quixote" by Cervantes. (Knopf). Below left: FRITZ KREDEL from "Hans Christian Andersen." (Limited Editions). Right: WILLIAM SHARP from "The Brothers Karamazov" by Fyodor Dostoyevsky. (Modern Library, Random House).

GORDON GRANT from "The Eternal Sea" by W. M. Williamson. (Coward-McCann). Below:
FREDERICK T. CHAPMAN from "The Wreck of the Wild Wave" by Edith Teacher Hind. (Oxford University Press).

FREDERICK T. CHAPMAN from "Iceland Fisherman" by Pierre Loti. (Knopf). Top right: GREGOR DUNCAN from "The Melforts Go to Sea" by Geraldine Pederson-Krag. (Holiday House). Bottom right: OSCAR OGG from "Introducing Charles Dickens" by May Lamberton Becker. (Dodd, Mead).

THOMAS HART BENTON from "Life on the Mississippi" by Mark Twain. (Limited Editions). Below: HOWARD SIMON from "Old Hell" by Emmet Gowan. (Modern Age).

Opposite Page: FEODOR ROJANKOVSKY from "Animal Stories" by Georges Duplaix. (Simon and Schuster).

THOMAS HANDFORTH from
"Mei Li." (Doubleday).

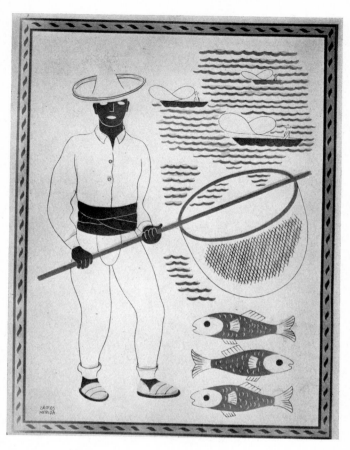

CARLOS MERIDA from his portfolio of "Native Costumes of Old Mexico." (Rudolf Lesch). Below: INGRI and EDGAR PARIN D'AULAIRE from their "Don't Count Your Chickens" and "Pocahontas" (Doubleday).

Opposite Page:

Left: INGRI and EDGAR PARIN D'AULAIRE from their "Washington." (Doubleday). Right: EDWARD A. WILSON from "The Rime of the Ancient Mariner" by Samuel Coleridge. (Limited Editions). Below: C. H. DEWITT from "The Story of New England" by Marshall McClintock. (Harpers).

THOMAS M. CLELAND from "Jonathan Wilde" by Henry Fielding. (Limited Editions). Above right: LYND WARD from "Robinson Crusoe" by Daniel Defoe. (Grosset and Dunlap). Bottom left: MASHA from "The Golden Almanac" by Dorothy A. Bennett. (Simon and Schuster). Bottom right: GRANT WOOD. Design used for the book jacket of "Oliver Wiswell" by Kenneth Roberts. (Doubleday).

THE MAN OF UZ

ARTHUR SZYK from "The Book of Job," taken from The Bible. (Heritage).

HENRY C. PITZ from "The Merchant of Venice" by William Shakespeare. (Folio Club). Below left: DONALD COOKE from his book, "Nutcracker of Nuremberg." (Winston).

105

From the shed roof, Mrs. Tarantino could look into . . .

GEORGE GROSZ from "1001 Afternoons in New York" by Ben Hecht. (Viking). Left: F. STROBEL from "Those Other People" by Mary King O'Donnell. (Houghton, Mifflin). Below: SAUL STEINBERG from his book, "Chucklebait." (Knopf).

CONSTANTIN ALAJÁLOV from "Outside Eden" by Isabel Scott Rorick. (Houghton, Mifflin). Below: from "Our Hearts Were Young and Gay," by Cornelia Otis Skinner and Emily Kimbrough. (Dodd, Mead).

Above and left: GLUYAS WILLIAMS from "Hear! Hear!" by William Freeman. (Harpers).

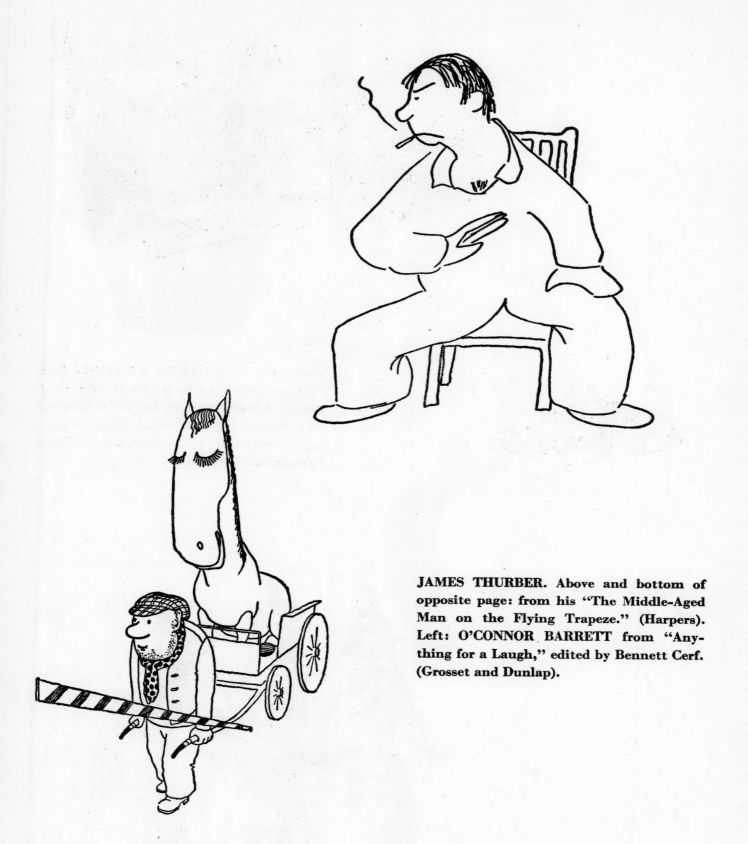

JAMES THURBER. Above and bottom of opposite page: from his "The Middle-Aged Man on the Flying Trapeze." (Harpers). Left: O'CONNOR BARRETT from "Anything for a Laugh," edited by Bennett Cerf. (Grosset and Dunlap).

Above and left: GARTH WILLIAMS from "Stuart Little" by E. B. White. (Harpers). Below: WILLIAM PÈNE DU BOIS from his "The Great Geppy." (Viking). Opposite Page, top: LUDWIG BEMELMANS from his "Hotel Bemelmans." (Viking).

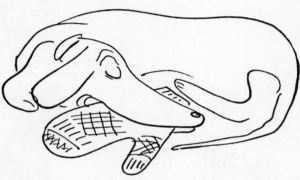

Right: LUDWIG BEMELMANS from his "Hansi." (Viking). Below left: WILLIAM STEIG from his "The Lonely Ones"—"*I recreated myself.*" (Duell, Sloane). Below right: KURT WIESE from "Freddy and Mr. Camphor" by Walter R. Brooks. (Knopf).

ROBERT LAWSON from "Ferdinand the Bull" by Munroe Leaf. (Viking). Bottom left: MILO WINTER from "Animal Inn" by Virginia Moe. (Houghton, Mifflin). Bottom right: GRACE PAULL from "Mr. Bumps and his Monkey" by Walter de la Mare. (Story Parade).

TIBOR GERGELY from "A Day in the Jungle" by Janette Sebring Lowrey. (Simon and Schuster).

GUSTAF TENGGREN from "Farm Stories" by K. and B. Jackson. (Simon and Schuster).

Two illustrations by GUSTAF TENGGREN from "Farm Stories" by K. and B. Jackson. (Simon and Schuster).

Below: GUSTAF TENGGREN from "Tenggren's Story Book." (Simon and Schuster).

Above: PAUL LANTZ from "The Matchlock Gun" by Walter D. Edmonds. (Dodd, Mead).
Below: TIBOR GERGELY from "Noah's Ark" by Jane Werner. (Grosset and Dunlap).

SALVADOR DALI from "The Autobiography of Benvenuto Cellini." (Doubleday).

SALVADOR DALI from "The Autobiography of Benvenuto Cellini." (Doubleday).

Above and opposite page, bottom: VERA BOCK from "Oscar Wilde Fairy Tales." (Peter Pauper). Below: FRITZ KREDEL from "The Decameron" by Giovanni Boccaccio. (Heritage).

VALENTI ANGELO from "The Long Christmas" by Ruth Sawyer (Viking) and (right) from "The Song of Songs, Which is Solomon's," taken from the Bible. (Heritage).

GEOFFREY HOLME from his "American Studio Paint Books," Volume I. (American Studio). **HENRIETTA JONES** from "A Pocket Full of Rhymes," compiled by Kathleen Love. (Crowell). Right: **PHOEBE NICOL** from "The Cordon Bleu Cook Book" by Dione Lucas. (Little, Brown).

BORIS ARTZYBASHEFF from his "The Seven Simeons" (Viking) and (below) from "Droll Stories," thirty tales by Balzac translated into modern English by Jacques Le Clercq. (Heritage).

BORIS ARTZYBASHEFF from "Droll Stories," thirty tales by Balzac translated into modern English by Jacques Le Clercq. (Heritage).

122

This is the DOG,
That worried the cat,
That killed the rat, that ate the malt,
That lay in the house that Jack built.

This is the COW with the crumpled horn,
That tossed the dog, that worried the cat,
That killed the rat, that ate the malt,
That lay in the house that Jack built.

BARBARA COONEY from "The Blot" by
Phyllis Crawford. (Holt). Below and right:
ROGER DUVOISIN from "Mother Goose"
by William Rose Benét. (Heritage).

This is the MAIDEN all forlorn,
That milked the cow with the crumpled horn,
That tossed the dog, . . . that worried the cat,
That killed the rat, . . . that ate the malt,
That lay in the house that Jack built.

21

124

NORMAN ROCKWELL from "Huckleberry Finn" by Mark Twain. (Heritage).

Opposite Page, top left: HELENE CARTER from "Twenty Little Pets from Everywhere" by Raymond L. Ditmars. (Messner). Top right: NURA from her book, "Nura's Children Go Visiting." (Studio). Bottom: DOROTHY P. LATHROP from her book, "Bouncing Betsy." (Macmillan). Above right: LEONARD WEISGARD from "The Little Island" by Golden MacDonald. (Doubleday). Below left: RUTH GANNET from her book, "Hi-Po, the Hippo." (Random House). Right: BOYD HANNA from "Poems of Longfellow." (Limited Editions). Bottom right: HENRY STAHLHUT from "Koos the Hottentot" by Josef Marias. (Knopf).

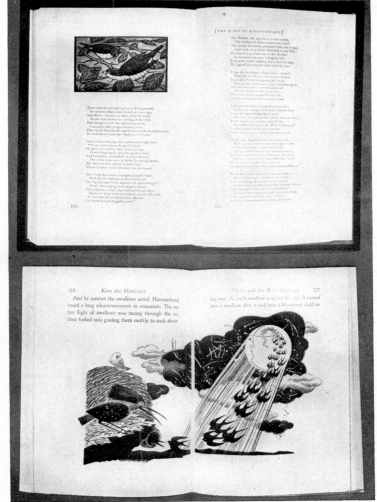

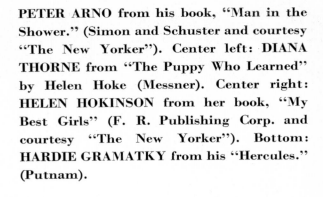

PETER ARNO from his book, "Man in the Shower." (Simon and Schuster and courtesy "The New Yorker"). Center left: DIANA THORNE from "The Puppy Who Learned" by Helen Hoke (Messner). Center right: HELEN HOKINSON from her book, "My Best Girls" (F. R. Publishing Corp. and courtesy "The New Yorker"). Bottom: HARDIE GRAMATKY from his "Hercules." (Putnam).

I'm punishing myself for being a naughty girl yesterday at Schraffts.